Feng Shui
for Home SALE

Easy ~ Practical ~ Effective

Alex Hartwell
Rhainey Watts-Cunningham

HenschelHAUS Publishing, Inc.
Milwaukee, Wisconsin

Published by
HenschelHAUS Publishing, Inc.
www.henschelHAUSbooks.com

ISBN: 978159598-544-6
E-ISBN: 978159598-730-3
LCCN: 2017905940

Illustrations / Diagrams by Alexis Ruzell

A portion of the proceeds from the sale of this book
goes to support homeless shelters.

What others are saying about *Feng Shui for Home SALE:*

"My father had a home that wouldn't sell due to the many problems with the home, plus my father's fear around letting it go. Feng Shui cures helped to sell the house and ease his anxiety."
—Theresa Reed

"Using Feng Shui helped sell our summer home quickly, we had multiple offers, and sold much above the asking price."
—Pam Stewart

"My home was on the market for a long time. When I used Feng Shui cures, I had an immediate response from buyers and sold my home."
—Jon Bartlett

"I sold my home 'For Sale By Owner' using inexpensive Feng Shui cures and sold before other houses in my neighborhood."
—Michelle Kahn

"Our realtor insisted on using Feng Shui cures, along with staging, to list our home. We balked at first, but were happy with the results."
—Jenny and Mark

"We had to relocate our family quickly due to a job change. It wasn't until we used Feng Shui that things came together smoothly."
—Kevin Williams

Contents

Foreword

My fascination with Feng Shui started in the early 90s while I was living in New York City and studying Feng Shui at the Open Center. I was excited, when after moving to Milwaukee and starting my real estate career in 2006, to meet Rhainey and Alex and discover their unique Feng Shui approach.

I am honored to introduce this book to you. It is a thoughtful approach to using Feng Shui to sell a home. The process has been tested and proven to be successful on dozens of houses listed and sold by our team in the past decade.

As I look back to each house sold with Feng Shui, I recall many things from how comfortable people felt at an open house to a special cure that brought an offer the next day. It is meaningful to me that this book highlights the conscious, focused use of intention. The use of intention, along with the Feng Shui cures, allows for higher sale prices and quicker and easier sales.

I invite you to enjoy this step-by-step methodology of selling a house that Rhainey and Alex have shared with us. Welcome to the world of Feng Shui and happy selling!

—Alexis Ruzell, Five Star Realtor

Alexisrealtygroup.com

Preface

Today, there is a growing awareness of systems and methods, like Reiki, acupuncture, yoga, meditation, sound healing and biofeedback, that utilize "energy" not currently measurable with scientific means. In Feng Shui, this unseen energy is referred to as *chi* or *life force energy*.

Feng Shui uses cures and adjustments to modify this kind of energy in order to bring about balance, harmony, and desired changes in someone's life. Feng Shui can be compared to acupuncture, in that energy pathways in the home are similar to energy meridians in the body. Feng Shui cures can be related to acupuncture needles; both are strategically placed to modify the energy flow, increase vitality, and support positive changes.

People are now more open to Feng Shui and other energy-based systems than ever before, as they look for ways to bring balance to their lives and better align with that part of themselves that creates a life of connection and ease.

We would like to thank our home sale and realtor clients who have entrusted us with the sale of their homes or other properties. Our experiences with them have helped us write this book.

Thank you,

Alex Hartwell

Rhainey Watts-Cunningham

Introduction

This book was written to provide simple and easy steps for you to best prepare your home for an optimal sale. As Feng Shui professionals, we have received extensive feedback over the years from realtors and homeowners that a "Feng Shui-ed" property sells more quickly and closer to listing price than homes that are not.

Feng Shui makes a unique contribution to the home sale process by focusing on energy flow and balance, rather than the physical appearance of a home, as staging does. The Feng Shui effect is to energetically attract more buyers to the home, invite more positive attention to the property, and smooth out the entire selling process. Feng Shui can create interest in a property and reduce objections a buyer might have. In addition, utilizing Feng Shui can result in higher sales prices from buyers who value your property that much more.

In the following chapters, we introduce nine basic areas of focus—or steps, along with adjustments that are easy and inexpensive to implement by the homeowner or realtor.

These have been selected as the most productive in generating a quick and profitable home sale.

Feng Shui for Home Sale devotes a chapter to each of these areas, describing potential problems and how to fix them. Examples in the book of problems in these areas are just a few of the many possible ways issues could manifest through imbalances.

Chapter 1 is devoted to Run-thrus, one of the more serious Feng Shui problems a home can have.

Chapter 2 and 3 introduce the ideas of Physical and Electrical Balance to a space.

Chapter 4 looks at the Bagua as a tool to help with restoring balance to a home.

Chapter 5 looks at Elemental Balance.

Chapters 6 and 7 explore singular elements, such as stairways and angles, as potentially detrimental to energy flow within a home.

Chapter 8 examines the exterior of the space, including its entry ways and the balance of the lot.

Chapter 9 covers the selection and installation of cures and enhancements.

The final chapters discuss useful ideas to use along with Feng Shui, as well as additional considerations.

When reading this book and benefiting from the information presented, it is helpful to have or create a floor plan of your own space. The legend below identifies items used to represent cures and items.

Our hope is that homeowners and realtors alike will begin to incorporate Feng Shui into the home sale process with successful results. In addition to guiding you through the process, our intent is to help demystify Feng Shui and make it easy and enjoyable for you to utilize, implement and understand.

Have Fun!

Legend of Symbols Used in this Book

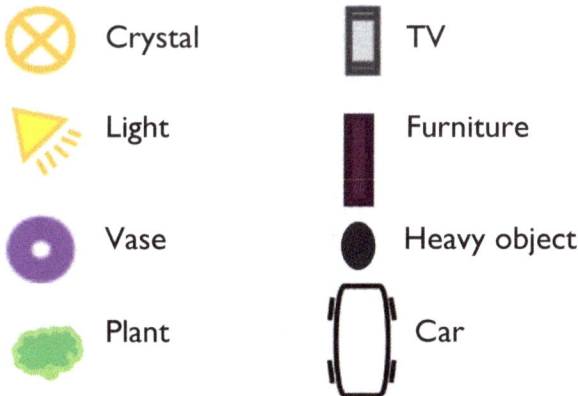

Crystal

Light

Vase

Plant

TV

Furniture

Heavy object

Car

Fig. 1. Ideal Site

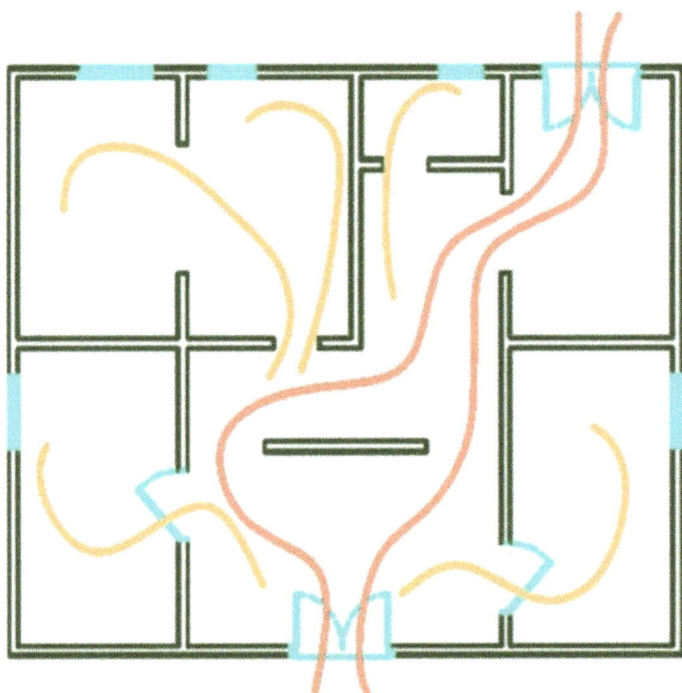

Fig. 2. Meandering Energy

Chapter 1
Run-thrus—The Primary Issue

O riginally, Feng Shui developed from a search for the ideal location for farmland in China. The search entailed evaluating the surrounding topography and geography of a site for the contribution of its physical and energetic components. An ideal site was considered to be a home situated halfway up a hill, facing south, overseeing a river (Fig. 1). This kind of site would allow for nourishment of the land from optimal sunshine, easy access to water, and protection from harsh winds. Over time, that process of looking at a property has been translated into methods of assessing a present-day home site.

Ideally, energy moves like a gentle meandering river throughout a home or property, nourishing every part of it equally (Fig. 2). In analyzing a home site today, we look at the degree to which the energy moves in this way.

Many Feng Shui corrections are directly related to problems with the flow of this energy. The most serious of these issues we describe as a "Run-thru." A Run-thru is a straight and uninterrupted pathway where energy moves too rapidly through a home. Looking at Run-thrus and energy pathways is the first step we take to Feng Shui a home.

The most significant or Primary Run-thru in a home occurs when the back door or a back window is directly opposite the front door and the pathway between the two is unobstructed (Fig. 3). The Run-thru creates a rushing river

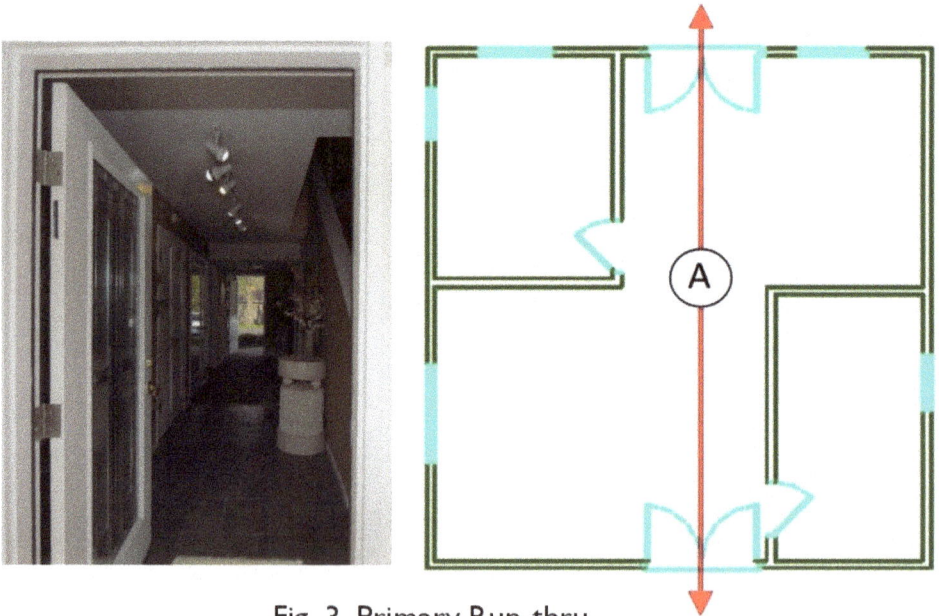

Fig. 3. Primary Run-thru

effect, which drains energy and vitality from the surrounding rooms, as well as energy from the homeowner's life. When the energy flows in the front door and out the back door or window in this way, it doesn't nourish other parts of the home, draining resources like money, support, and relationship. Also, clutter can gather as the homeowners unconsciously try to ground themselves and slow the energy of the river effect down by placing objects in and around the pathway.

In correcting or "curing" a Run-thru, the intent is to interrupt the rushing energy so that it meanders and nourishes more of the home for the home sale. The nourishment then can support the flow of money and improve relationships, benefiting the home sale. Clutter that is no longer being used to modify the Run-thru is managed more easily for showings.

Fig. 4. Secondary Run–thru

Other types of Run-thrus, called Secondary Run-thrus, occur when there is an interior door opposite a window, or two windows opposite each other (Fig. 4). Additionally, a Run-thru is created when an uninterrupted hallway or space is 30 feet or longer. These Run-thrus affect the life areas of the home that they are involved with (Fig. 5). Specifically, if they occur in the Wealth, Health, Relationship or Helpful People Areas, they are of greater concern for the home sale. (See Bagua, Chapter 4).

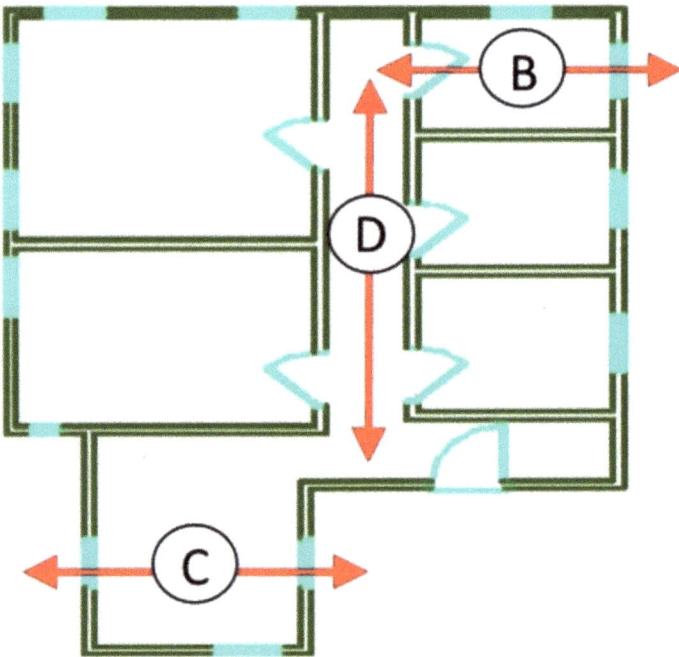

Fig. 5. Secondary Run-thrus

The traditional Feng Shui interrupter for a Primary Run-thru is to hang a faceted crystal ball in the Run-thru pathway (Fig. 6). Other ways to adjust the energy flow include placing furniture, large plants, pots, decorative screens, a substantial object, an area rug, lighting, artwork or a combination of smaller items like large flower vases in and along the pathway (Fig. 7). These items are placed in a way that requires the energy to move around them, redirecting the flow to create a gentle winding effect, like the meandering river.

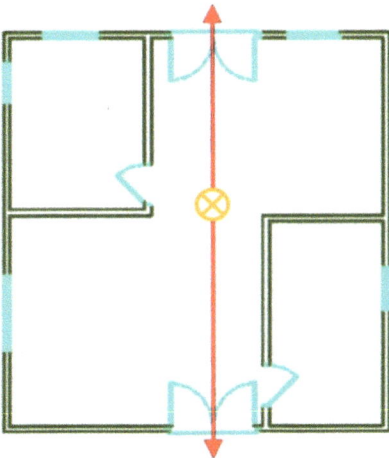

Fig. 6. Primary Run-thru
Crystal Cure

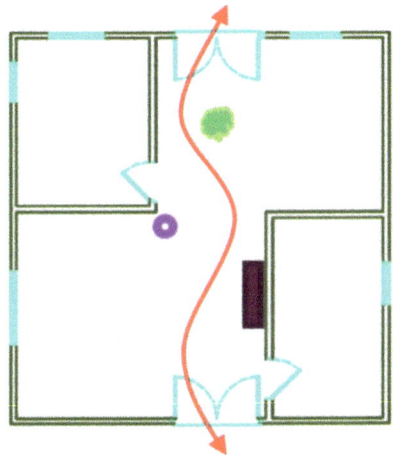

Fig. 7. Primary Run-thru
Other Cures

Secondary Run-thrus are treated in the same way, using small items and smaller crystals (Fig. 8 and 9).

Fig. 8. Secondary Run-thru Other Cures

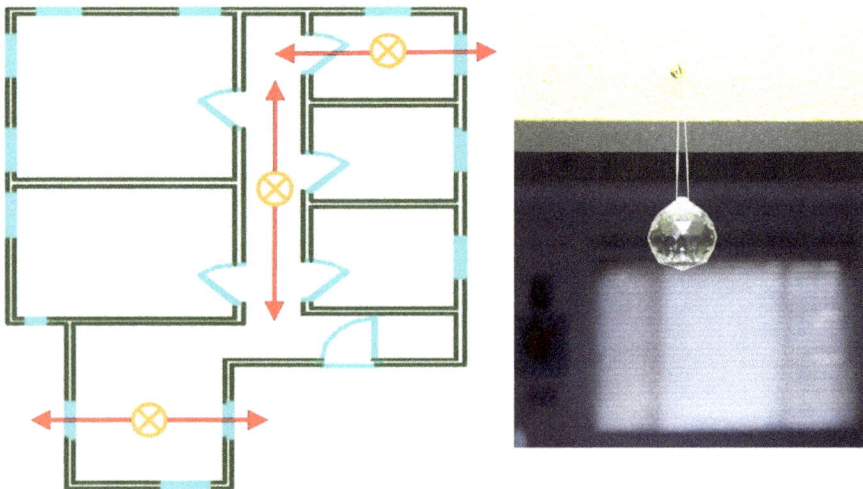

Fig. 9. Secondary Run-thru Crystal Cures

In some primary Run-thru situations, grounding objects placed at the wall edges of the Run-thru, opposite one another and about half the length of the Run-thru, can be used to modify the flow of energy. (Fig. 9a).

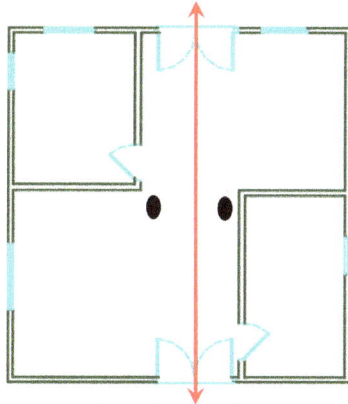

Fig. 9a: Heavy Objects

Frequently, we encounter homeowners who tell us they have read Feng Shui books and have tried to apply what they have read. In most cases, we find they miss significant issues like Run-thrus. For example, a homeowner called us and asked for our help, because he was still struggling to sell his home after making Feng Shui adjustments from what he had read.

Immediately upon walking into the home, it was clear to us that there was an unobstructed Run-thru from the front door to the back door without any corrections. Soon after installing the cures, the homeowners had three showings and a viable offer.

Adjusting or curing Run-thrus, if they are present, is essential to a successful home sale. However, in some cases, Run-thrus can be of benefit and may not need treatment. For example, a Run-thru that separates a guest room from the rest of the house could be desirable for a buyer seeking a feeling of privacy from their guests.

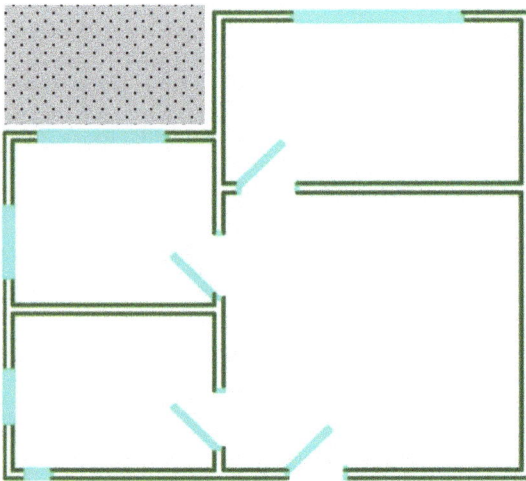

Fig. 10. Missing Area

Chapter 2
Missing Areas and Extensions

Restoring balance is central to the Feng Shui process. We see a direct relationship between restoring the balance of a home and generating a successful home sale. In Feng Shui, we look at balance in terms of the Structural, Electrical and Activity aspects of a home. Structural items include Missing Areas, Extensions, Run-thrus, stairways, angled walls and ceilings, garges, bathrooms, and Shar points.

We begin with the floor plan of the home to see if there are Missing Areas or Extensions. These are important structural issues to consider.

A Missing Area is created when a home shape or floor plan is less than an exact square or rectangle and the length of the missing space is less than one half of the length of the wall it is on (Fig. 10).

An Extension is created by the portion of the home that is left when the length of the missing space is more than one half of the wall it is on (Fig. 11).

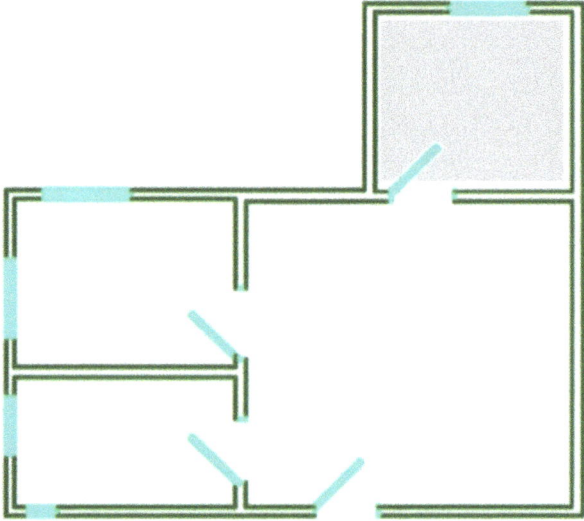

Fig. 11. Extension

Imbalances occur in a home because a Missing Area or Extension disrupts the even flow of energy in the rest of the home. Cures are used in both cases so that the Missing Area is not a detriment and so that the Extension can become a benefit.

In the case of a Missing Area (Fig. 10), a cure would be used to fill in the energy of the missing space (Fig. 12). The cure most frequently used, because it is inexpensive and easy to install, is a leaded, faceted crystal ball. The ball is hung nine inches down from the ceiling and three to nine inches out from the center of one or both of the Missing Area walls. For larger Missing Areas, it is best to cure both walls.

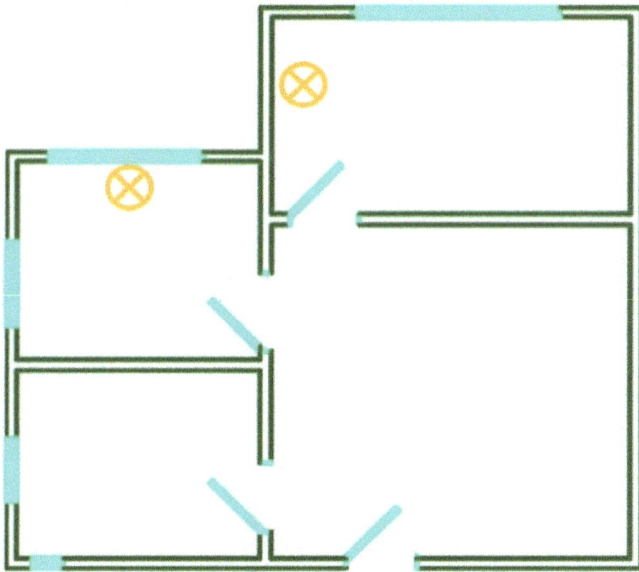

Fig. 12. Missing Area Crystal Cure

The Missing Area can also be filled in by placing a light shining back on the house exactly at the outside corner of the Missing Area (Fig. 13). Alternatively, an energizing element, like a tree, a garden, a sitting area, a large fountain, sculpture or bird-feeding area can be placed in the Missing Area.

Fig. 13. Missing Area Light Cure

In the case of an Extension (Fig. 11), a cure would be used to raise the energy of the area opposite the Extension (Fig. 14). Again, the crystal is the simplest cure and would be placed within the area equal to the size of the extension and opposite of it.

Alternatively, energetic objects, ranging from a plant to a lamp, could be placed in the same area. Cures placed at these points balance the energy of the extension. For a list of other energizing objects or cures, see Appendix A.

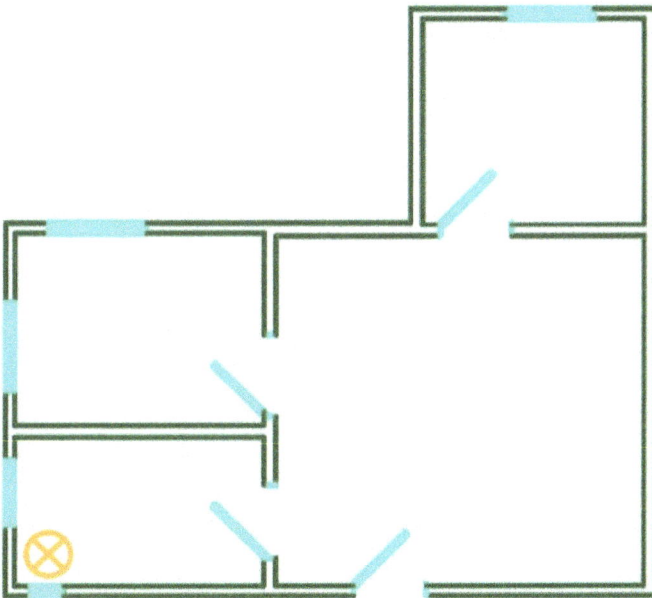

Fig. 14. Extension Crystal Cure

Figures 15 and 16 show how Feng Shui looks at which rooms are opposite of each other when considering balance. Opposites are perpendicular when in the center and diagonal when in the corners.

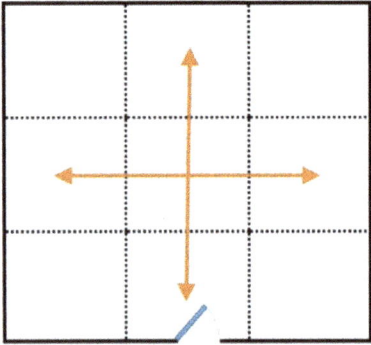

Fig. 15. Perpendicular
Opposites

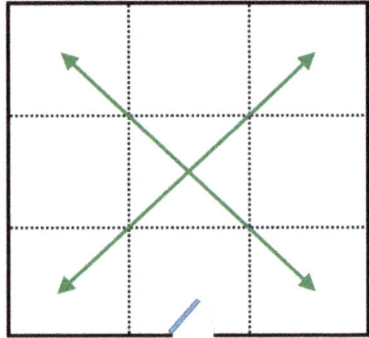

Fig. 16. Diagonal
Opposites

When structural cures are not making enough of a difference in accomplishing client goals, a crystal can be used in the center of the home to help balance out energetic differences that aren't easily quantifiable.

In one case, a family had lived in their home for 17 years without issues until they built a kitchen addition. After the remodel was complete, they began to have financial troubles that continued until their home fell into foreclosure. When they attempted to sell the home, their realtor called us to help with the sale. After studying the floor plans before and after the remodel (Fig. 17 and 18), we discovered that the remodel floor plan created a Missing Area in Wealth. (See Chapter 4, Bagua Life Areas.)

Cures were utilized to correct the Missing Area and helped to complete the home sale. An earlier solution could have addressed the Feng Shui problem in the first place and allowed them to keep their house.

Achieving a healthy balance can help create interest in a home or property and highlight its positive aspects. Ease of

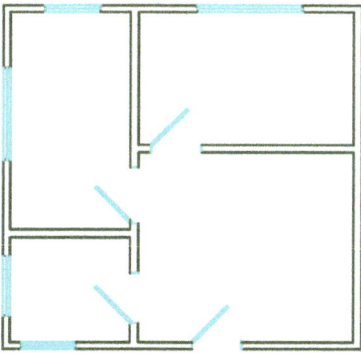

Fig. 17. Before Remodel

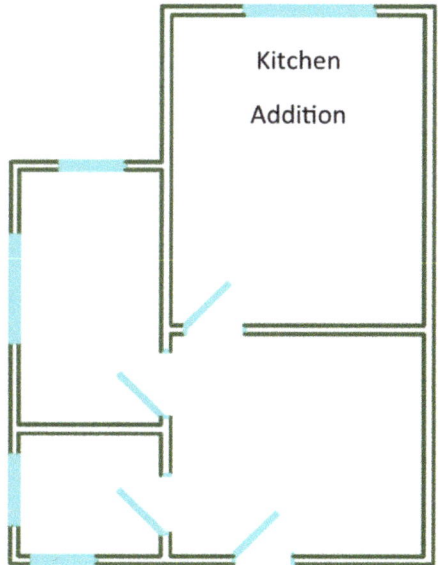

Kitchen

Addition

Fig. 18. After Remodel

sale and obtaining the optimal sale price for the property are other benefits of healthy home balance.

Other Structural Elements, including Angles, Bathrooms, Stairs, Garages, and Shars, are discussed in Chapters 6 and 7.

Notes

....

....

....

....

....

....

....

....

....

....

....

....

Chapter 3
Balancing Activity and
Electrical Components

L ooking at the balance of Activity and Electrical levels is also important. Some examples of Activities in a home include cooking, eating, reading, sleeping and kids playing. Electrical examples include anything that is plugged in, like a lamp, a television, computer or microwave.

Imbalances occur when there are differences in Activity or Electrical levels in any of the opposite areas (Fig. 15 and 16). Again, as with Structural Balance, Chapter 2, the room oppositions are considered either as diagonally opposite or perpendicularly opposite each other in the house when viewing the floor plan.

Because of their energizing quality, Electrical and Activity elements need to be considered in terms of balance. For example, an imbalance of Activity occurs

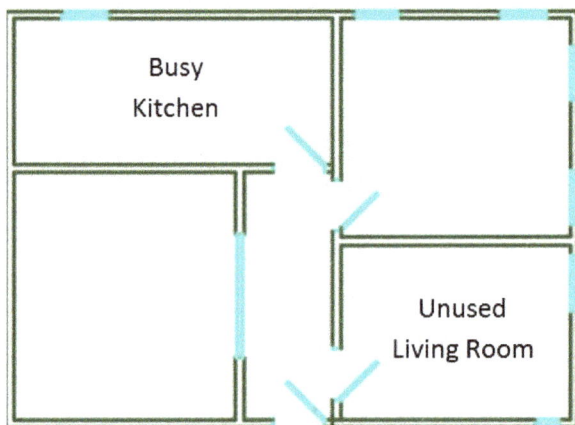

Fig. 19. Activity Imbalance

when an active eat-in kitchen is opposite an unused living room (Fig. 19).

An Electrical Imbalance occurs when a quiet study with a single lamp is opposite a rec room with a large television (Fig. 20). Most often, rooms have both Electrical and Activity levels involved and the balance of the combination of both needs to be taken into account. Generally,

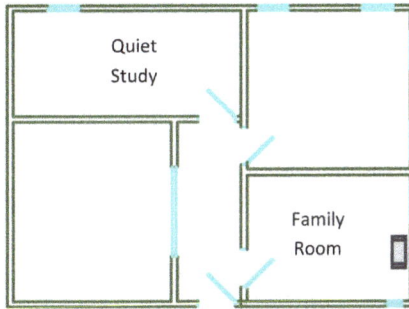

Fig. 20. Electrical Imbalance

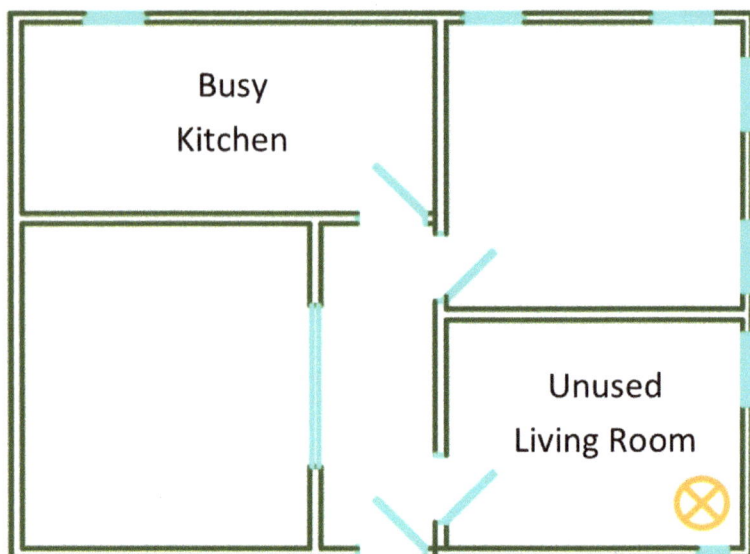

Fig. 21. Activity Imbalance Crystal Cure

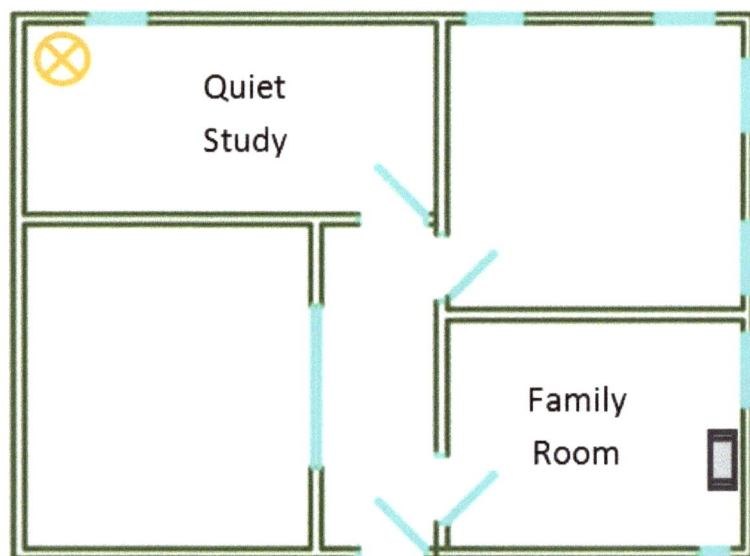

Fig. 22. Electrical Imbalance Crystal Cure

kitchens will have higher Electrical and Activity elements compared to most rooms opposing them.

Activity and Electrical levels should also be evaluated in terms of frequency and intensity. For example, a home owner who only cooks on Sundays and eats out the rest of the week, would demonstrate low cooking activity, whereas a family of four who always cooks and eats at home, would be demonstrating a high cooking activity level. A large television frequently watched has a higher level of electrical intensity than a small computer occasionally used.

Further examples of activities that might be considered in the home include animals kept in one area, bathroom activity or workshop areas. Electrical examples can also include stoves, fish tanks and air conditioners.

To cure Activity imbalances, the energy of the less active room is raised. This can be accomplished by hanging a crystal (Fig. 21). Alternatively, a light, electrical item or other cures listed in Appendix A can be used in the less active room. To cure Electrical imbalances, raise the energy of the room with less electrical charge in the same way by using a crystal (Fig. 22) or cures listed in Appendix A. Looking at activity levels becomes less important when the seller is no longer living in the home.

We visited a home for sale that had received limited attention from real estate agents and potential buyers. The home had an active family room with a large television set opposite an infrequently used dining room. We had the owners hang a 40mm crystal in the center of the room over the dining room table to assist in balancing the energy of the active family room.

After several weeks, we returned to the home and were told there had been more showings, but no offers had come in. We had the homeowners exchange the 40mm crystal with a larger 50mm crystal to further raise the energy of the dining room. This adjustment improved the balance and brought in several offers. The subtlety of the Electrical/Activity relationship, as in this case, can require testing and reevaluation.

When Activity and Electrical cures are not completely accomplishing client goals, a crystal can be used in the center of the home to help balance out energetic differences that aren't easily quantifiable.

While balancing the energy of the first floor is primary, it is also of value to consider doing the same for a second floor, if there is one.

Notes

....

....

....

....

....

....

....

....

....

....

....

....

....

....

....

....

....

....

....

....

....

....

WEALTH & PROSPERITY	FAME & REPUTATION	RELATIONSHIP & MARRIAGE
HEALTH & FAMILY	CENTER	CREATIVITY & CHILDREN
KNOWLEDGE & SELF-CULTIVATION	CAREER	HELPFUL PEOPLE & TRAVEL

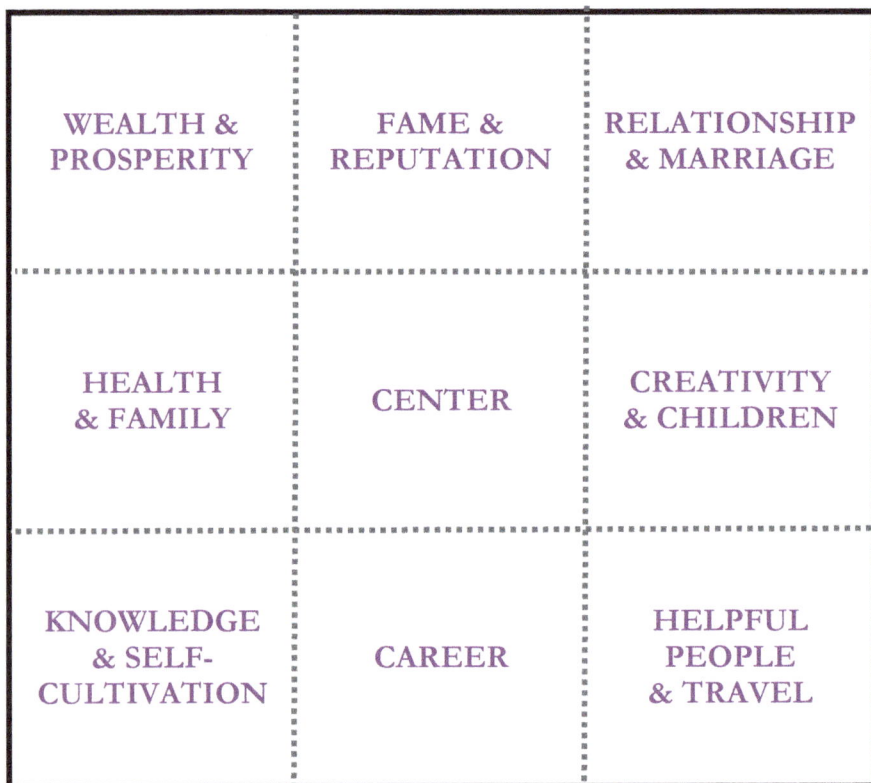

Fig. 23. Bagua Life Areas

Chapter 4
The Bagua

O ne of the major tools in Feng Shui is the Bagua, which was derived from the I-Ching. It is used to locate the Life Areas in the home and to focus related intentions in those areas (Fig. 23).

To find where the Life Areas are located in your home, place the Bagua map over the first floor of the home floor plan with the bottom edge in line with the main entry door of the house (Fig. 24 on page 32). (If you do not have a floor plan, draw one of your own that is to scale, in proportion, or a reasonable estimate.)

Next, line up the left side of the Bagua with the longest external wall on the left side of the house (Fig. 25 on page 32). Then stretch the Bagua to do the same, first on the right wall (Fig. 26 on page 33) and then on the back side of the house (Fig. 27 on page 33), matching the longest external wall in each case.

With the Bagua overlaying the floor plan in this way, you can see which Life Areas correspond to specific parts

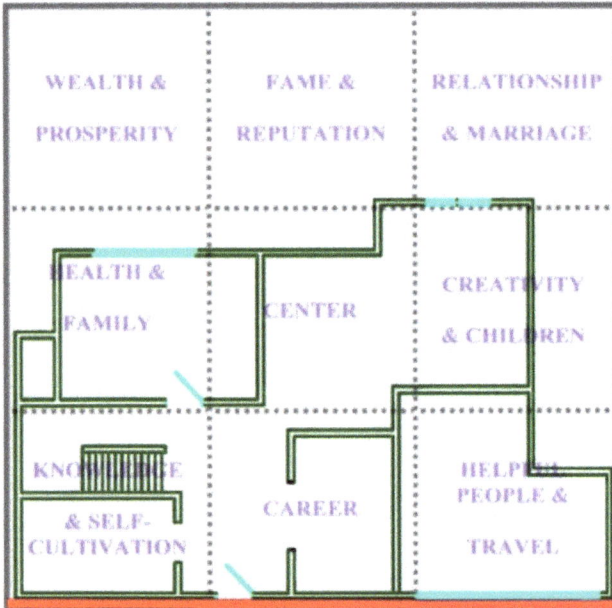

Fig. 24. Bagua in line with front door

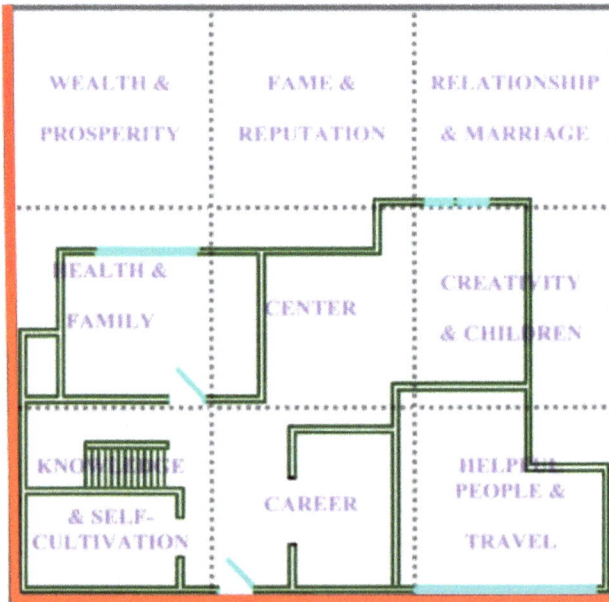

Fig. 25. Bagua left wall

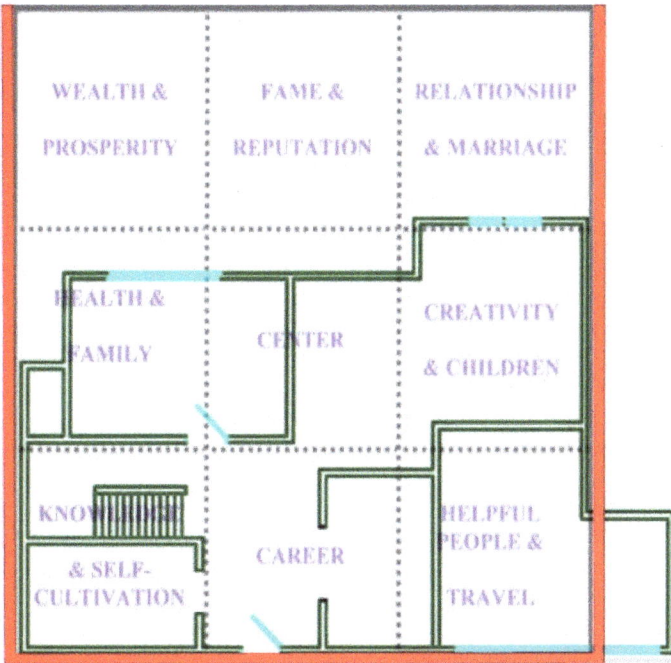

Fig. 26. Bagua right wall

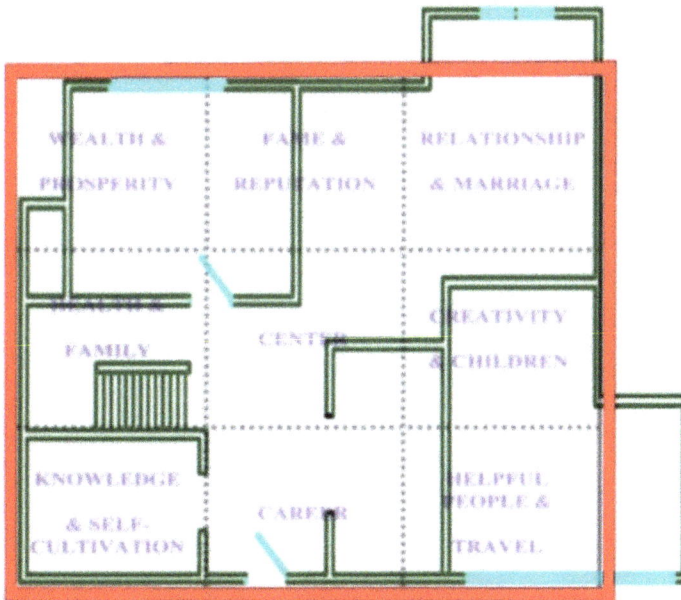

Fig. 27. Bagua back wall

of the home. You can also discover which Life Areas are related to a Missing Area (Fig. 28) and which areas are connected to an Extension (Fig. 29). Any portions of the Bagua that are not filled in by the house are considered Missing Areas.

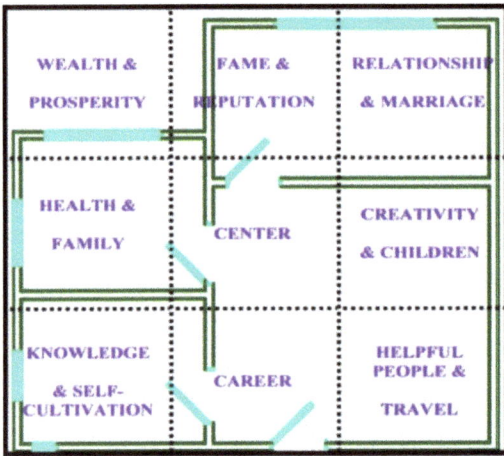

Fig. 28. Bagua Over Missing Area

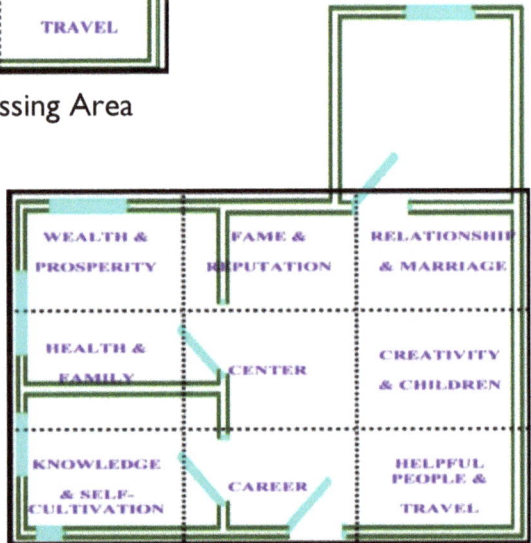

Fig. 29. Bagua Over Extension

Areas that extend out beyond the Bagua are considered Extensions. Knowing which Life Areas relate to the Missing sections or Extensions helps to see potential benefits or problems related to the home sale.

For example, a home that has an extension in the Fame Area could have an abundance of showings. If the Helpful People Area is extended, the sale process is likely to go more smoothly because of the abundance of help available.

Extensions can add value to the Life Areas they are connected to as long as they are in balance with their opposite area. If the home has an extension in Helpful People that is not in balance with its opposite area, Wealth, it could manifest as problems with the lender or buyer.

Missing Areas can detract value from the corresponding Life Areas if not cured. For example, if the home has a missing Wealth Area, it may sell at a lower price or not at all. If some of the Helpful People Area is missing, there could be frequent delays in the sale process because of lack of cooperation among the people involved.

Key Life Areas that are most important to home sale are Wealth, Fame, and Helpful People. Wealth relates to the home sale price and expenses involved in the home sale process. Fame corresponds to the level and quality of attention the property receives. Helpful People relates to how cooperative and supportive bankers, realtors, buyers, and others involved in the process can be.

The Bagua can also be overlaid on the floor plan of the home to explore which Life Areas are affected by Electrical elements or Activity levels. Life Areas that have significant Electrical or Activity levels are energized. For example, kitchens are generally more active than other areas of the house. Having a kitchen in the Fame Area could draw more potential buyers to the home. Family rooms can have large televisions that activate the Life Area in which they are located. If you find one in Helpful People, it could indicate better relationships across the board—from home inspectors to title companies and appraisers.

It is important to note that higher Electrical and Activity levels are beneficial only if they are in balance with their opposite area. For example, if the home has an often-used computer room in Wealth, but the area opposite is unused, it could manifest as an average to low sale price or low-ball offers due to the imbalance.

Although we have discussed Key Life Areas, it is important to note that the other Life Areas can have impact as well and should be examined for the degree to which they affect the home sale. For example, when selling the family home, it is useful to pay attention to the Health and Family area to create a comfortable sense of belonging in the buyer. The home sale process can be stressful and might put a strain on a marriage or relationship, so a healthy Relationship Area can support better communication.

The Center section of the Bagua is also important as it relates to all of the Life Areas and can benefit or detract from the home sale. Oftentimes, the center of a home lacks a grounded focus, which can detract from the owner's intent.

To adjust for this and stabilize the home, bring an item or items to the Center Area that carry some weight to them or give an impression of heaviness, like a potted plant or large floor vase. Additionally, an area rug or valued picture can be used to bring focus to the Center Area. If that is not feasible, a crystal can be hung in the approximate center of the home.

Looking at the Bagua Life Areas that are currently presenting difficulty or challenges to the home sale can provide you with information on where imbalances may be present in the home and help you determine where cures might be needed to help with the home sale.

The Bagua can also be overlaid on the lot of the home, which will be discussed in Chapter 8. The important role elements play in your space as they relate to Life Areas is discussed in the next chapter.

Fire
RED

WEALTH & PROSPERITY	FAME & REPUTATION	RELATION-SHIP & MARRIAGE
HEALTH & FAMILY	CENTER *Earth* EARTH TONES	CREATIVITY & CHILDREN
KNOWLEDGE & SELF-CULTIVATION	CAREER	HELPFUL PEOPLE & TRAVEL

Wood
GREENS

Metal
WHITE
SILVER

Water
BLUE, BLACK

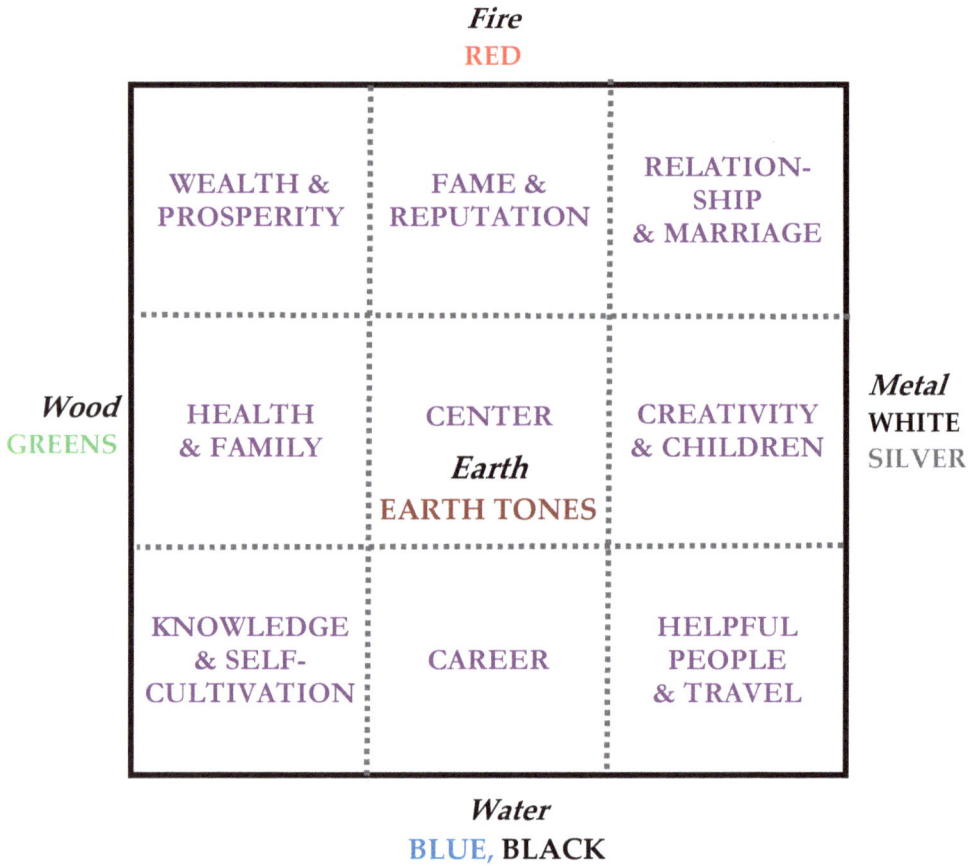

Fig. 30. Bagua with Elements

Chapter 5
Elemental Balance

The five elements represent the natural forces that can combine and interact in our lives in a beneficial or problematic way. They include Wood, Fire, Metal, Earth and Water.

- Wood element items include plants, flowers, trees, green colors and rectangles.

- The Fire element is represented by the colors red, bright orange, and bright yellow, as well as triangles and fire itself.

- Blues, blacks, wavy lines and water represent the Water element.

- The Metal element is represented by circles, the colors white and silver and Metal objects.

- Unglazed pottery, dirt, squares and earth tone colors represent the Earth element. (See Appendix A for more information on the elements.)

A home that has some representation of all of the elements is more attractive to buyers. Occasionally, one element may be dominant in a home. For example, a home with green décor, wood paneling and many plants, has a dominant wood element. This may create an unbalanced feeling. It could be equally uncomfortable if one element is significantly lacking. For example, a home that has no earth representations could feel less grounded for the buyers.

Adjustments to the above examples and others can be managed by utilizing the Creative Cycle (Fig. 31) or Destructive Cycle of elements (Fig. 32).

The two cycles show the order in which individual elements enhance or reduce each other. If the Wood element is dominant in your home, look to the Destructive Cycle to see which element minimizes the effect of Wood. Metal is used to mediate the effect of Wood, so in this case, bring in metal items, silver or white colors or circular patterns.

Alternatively, reduce the amount of wood in the home or, if possible, add the elements that are lacking in proportion to the wood to achieve balance.

In a case of too little Earth in proportion to the other elements in a home, add more of the Earth element or

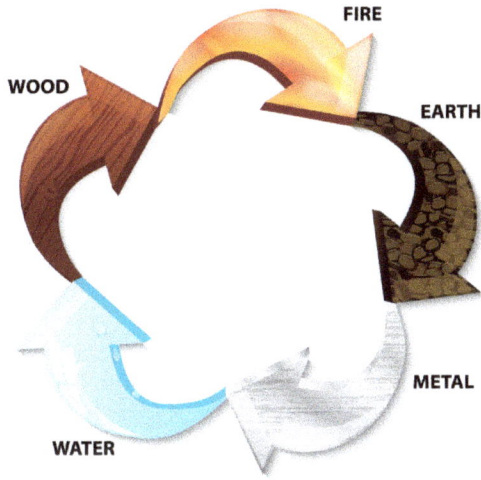

Fig. 31. Creative Cycle

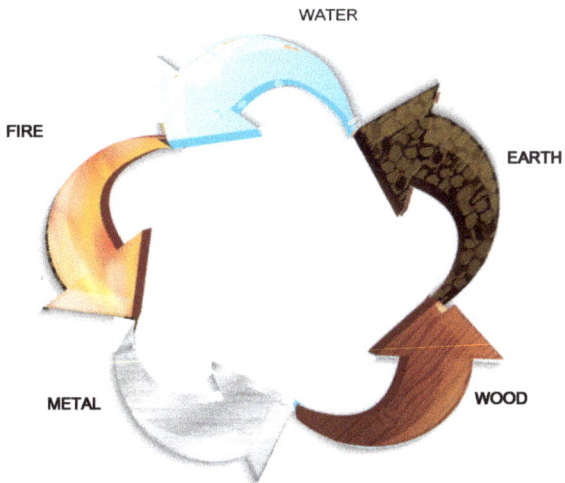

Fig. 32. Destructive Cycle

support it with its enhancing element from the Creative Cycle—Fire.

The elements Fire, Water, Earth, Metal, and Wood can be located on the Bagua map, along with their natural position and colors (Fig. 30 on page 38).

When selling a home, we look to see if there is an element placed in a way that might be in conflict with the natural element of that Life Area to the detriment of the home sale.

An important example is when the Water element is found in the Fame Area, whose natural element is Fire. Water in the form of fish tanks, sinks, fountains, extensive blue color or wavy lines placed in the Fame Area can extinguish its fire or create steam. Pictures of waterfalls, lakes and rivers may also be detrimental in the Fame Area and invite unfavorable attention to the home.

This can also be seen outdoors in the lot Bagua when a swimming pool, hot tub or pond is situated in the Fame Area (see Chapter 8).

Another example is fireplaces, which can be frequently found in the Health and Family Area, where the natural element is Wood. This conflict could create an uneasy feeling in the potential home buyer or reduce that "feel at home" sense you are trying to create in a home for sale. To balance misplaced elements, either remove the offending element or use the Creative or Destructive Cycle to mitigate its effect.

We were invited to visit a "For Sale by Owner" house that had been on the market for quite some time. Several offers had come in, but all had fallen apart for some reason or another. In evaluating the home, we discovered the Water element to be dominant.

A large fountain greeted us at the entry to the home. The interior colors were predominantly blue, artwork was dominated by images of the ocean, and mirrors were present throughout the home. Because mirrors are considered to be a Metal element, and Metal creates Water, these added to the water represented by the artwork and the blue interior.

We considered the excess water to be responsible for "washing away" the offers made on the home so far. After reducing the number of mirrors and bringing in plants to absorb some of the excess water, the owner received an accepted offer.

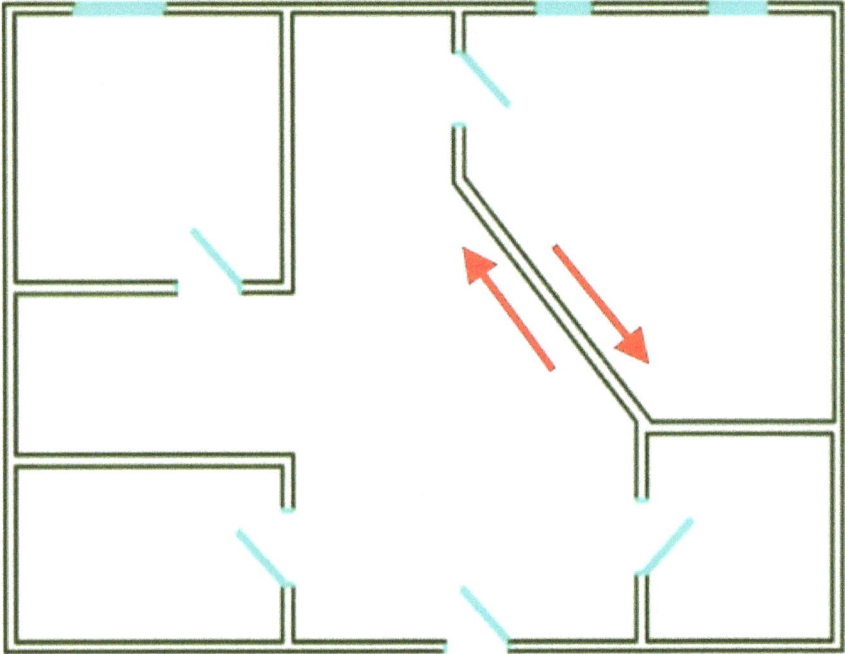

Fig. 33. Angled Walls

Chapter 6
Issues with
Angles and Shars

In our experience, angled walls, ceilings and doors can create significant Feng Shui problems for the Life Areas in which they occur. The energy along angled walls and ceilings flows more rapidly than along other walls, creating energetic imbalances within the entire home (Fig. 33).

Angles in the home tend to generate issues that are problematic or tricky. A special effort is made to correct them if they are in a Key Life Area. For example, an angled wall in Fame could manifest as mistakes being made in a home's marketing materials. An angled door in the Helpful People Area could show itself as someone in the home sale process being less than trustworthy.

Cures for the angled walls bring balance to the home by slowing down the speed of flow along the angled wall so that it is more in harmony with the rest of the room. To cure angled walls, place an object centered on the wall, or at each end of the wall. Use items such as paintings, decorative vases or potted plants (live or silk).

Another option is to hang a crystal centered on the wall three to nine inches out from the wall and three to nine inches down from the ceiling.

For an angled doorway, place tiles, plaques, stenciling or artwork of some kind above both sides of the door (Fig. 34). Another option is to hang a crystal on both sides of the door three inches out from the center of the door and three inches down.

In the case of an angled ceiling (Fig. 35), place pictures or items similar to those used with the angled door inter-

Fig. 34. Angled Door with Cure

mittently along the angled surface of the ceiling with the intent to visually open up the surface and make it feel less oppressive. An angled ceiling can also be cured by installing skylights, lighting, crystals or mobiles to interrupt the effect of the angle (Fig. 36).

Points and corners generate sharp, harmful energy or what is called *Shar Chi*. In Feng Shui, a *Shar* is created when a corner 90 degrees or less extends into a room (Fig. 37) or out from an exterior building (Fig. 39).

Fig. 35. Angled Ceiling

Fig. 36. Angled Ceiling Cured

Fig. 38. Shar Ceiling Edge

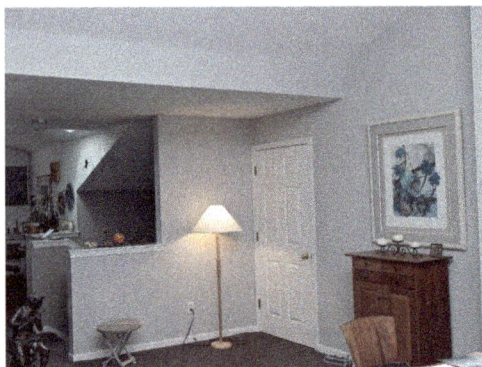

Fig. 37. Shar Corner

Other examples of Shars include pointed objects, sharp corners on furniture, or corners and edges created by changes in ceiling levels (Fig. 38). Energy extends directly out from the corner, point or edge like an arrow, negatively affecting whatever is in its path.

We look at interior Shars for their effect on Key Life Areas. Shars can create a variety of issues, ranging from lack of interest in the home on the part of buyers, discomfort when viewing the home, or trouble negotiating the sale.

We consider Shars created from exterior buildings or objects first, because they potentially have a stronger impact (Fig. 39). In Hong Kong, companies intentionally constructed buildings with Shars directed at their competitors' buildings in order to negatively affect those businesses. The practice got so out of hand that laws were passed against building in this way. Signage and sculpture are examples of outdoor Shars that could also be potentially harmful.

Interior Shars are cured by placing objects in front of the corners and points to block the arrow energy (Fig. 40). Items that can be used include plants, draped fabric, corner

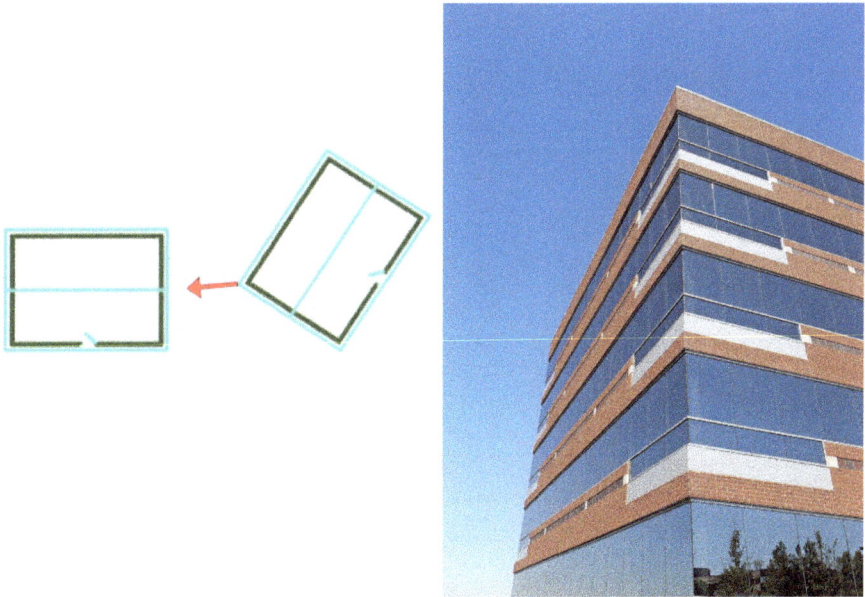

Fig. 39. Exterior Shar

protectors and so on. A crystal can also be hung from the ceiling off the Shar edge or point.

A change in ceiling level is cured by placing plaques, tiles, mirrors or other decorative items intermittently along the face of the drop down (Fig. 41). An exterior Shar is cured by placing an object in line with the Shar between the Shar and the house. In some cases, when larger Shars cannot be interrupted, a Bagua mirror (see Appendix A) is placed outside the home facing the offending Shar with the intent to block the energy.

Fig. 41. Dropped Ceiling Cure

Fig. 40. Shar Corner Cure

Chapter 7
Bathrooms, Garages and Stairways—Further Disruptions

BATHROOMS

Wherever a bathroom is located in the house, it drains energy from the corresponding Life Area, which can affect the home sale. For example, a bathroom in Wealth could drain away money when a home inspection reveals costly repairs that need to be made. A bathroom in Fame could relate to a pre-existing condition in the house that could damage the reputation of the property. A bathroom in the Helpful People Area could leave you, the home seller, as the only helpful person in the process, so that you end up doing most of the work to get your home sold.

A bathroom drain-out can be cured by hanging a crystal in the center of the bathroom to reverse the effect

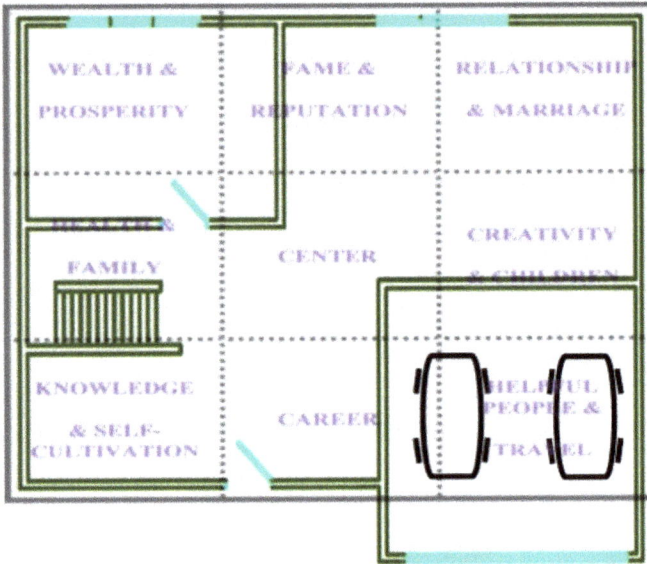

Fig. 42. Attached Garage

or by placing a full-length mirror on the outside of the bathroom door to "disappear" the draining effect of the bathroom.

GARAGES

The energy flow of an attached garage is often quite different from that of the rest of the home and can create imbalances within the home.

The attached garage is treated as part of the Bagua (Fig. 42). Each Life Area within the garage needs be treated for the in-and-out energy of the cars. In the case of home

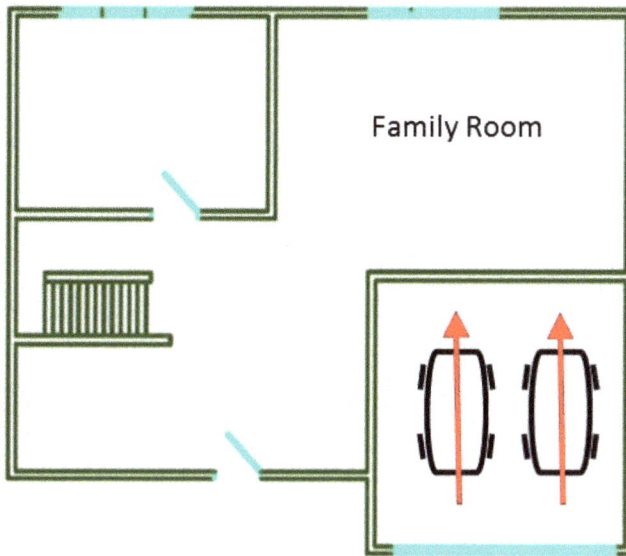

Fig 43. Car Energy into Home

sale, most of the time, an attached garage will relate to the Wealth or Helpful People areas. For example, a home with an attached garage in the Helpful People Area could mean buyers visiting, but not staying long enough to appreciate what the home has to offer.

When the attached garage includes Wealth, it could reduce the sale price or increase the costs of preparing the home for sale.

The easiest way to cure a garage is to hang a crystal in the center of each Life Area the garage covers. Curing an attached garage can bring balance to the Life Areas affected, as well as to the entire house.

The garage may be considered separate from the Bagua if there are steps from the main house to the garage, or if there is a Run-thru that disconnects the house and the garage.

Often, garages have incoming cars pointing towards an actively used space in the home (Fig. 43). This sends disruptive energy to that living space and could manifest as a buyer feeling less than comfortable when touring the home. There is less concern when the cars are directed at a laundry room, closet or mudroom.

For garages that have cars directed towards the living area, placing large heavy items such as tires, riding lawn mowers or filing cabinets between the house and the car is recommended. If there is too little space for objects, a crystal can be hung between the car and the house with the intent to block the incoming energy.

Garages can also be disruptive to activities in the rooms above them, especially bedrooms or rooms where calm focus is important. A buyer may sense this instability when touring the room. The in-and-out energy can be treated by hanging a crystal in the garage beneath the room, centered on that room's space with the intent to ground and calm the effect of the garage. Alternatively, a heavy object can be placed in the center of the room above the garage. If preferred, take two heavy objects and place one to either side above the garage entry door in that room.

STAIRWAYS

A stairway is looked at as energy draining out of an area. The most important example is when a second-floor stairway drains down and out the front door, taking with it energy and resources (Fig. 44).

This can manifest as energy pushing interested buyers away from the home or the homebuyer losing much of the support needed to complete the home sale. A basement

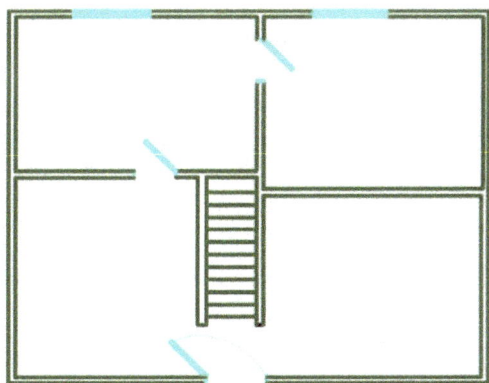

Fig. 44. Stairway Out Front Door

staircase relates to energy loss in the Life Area from which it originates. For example, a stairway to a lower level that begins in Fame could mean reduced attention being paid to the home.

Cures for stairways are intended to slow down or block the drain of energy. For example, a crystal can be placed centered on the stairs anywhere along its path. Pictures or wall hangings can also be used along the stairway to draw energy up (Fig. 45).

Another cure is a mirror at the top of the stairway, which has the same effect. In the case of a stairway aligned with the front door, a wind chime or crystal can be hung

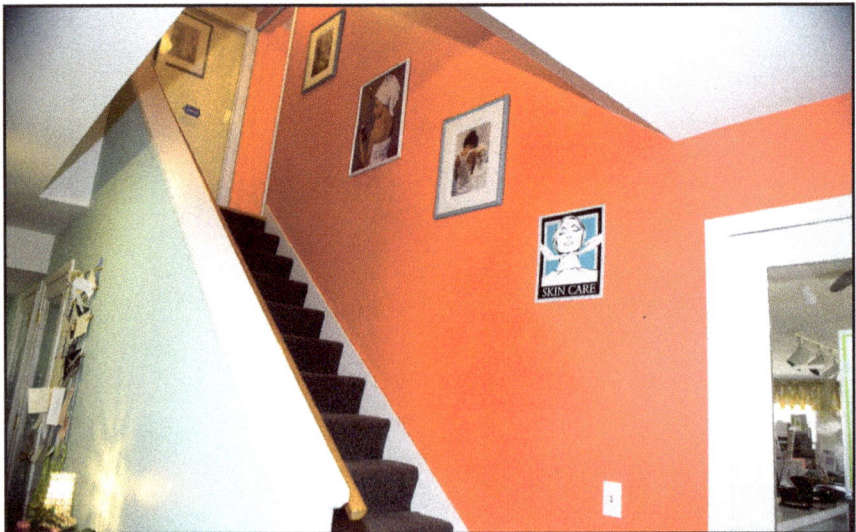

Fig. 45. Stairway Cure

between the foot of the stairs and the front door to stop the drain of energy and resources.

A bathroom situated at the top of the stairs is also a concern. Treat it by hanging a crystal in the center of the bathroom or between the bathroom and the top of the stairs, centered on the stairway.

A realtor contacted us when she had poor attendance at open houses for one of her listings. She said people would often stop or slow down to look, but rarely came inside. This was noticeably different from open houses she held at other locations, which were well attended. On our visit to the property, we had a hard time locating it and drove past several times. When we walked in the front door, the down-rushing energy of the staircase facing the front door showed us how potential buyers were being pushed away from seeing the property. When the cure—a wind chime at the bottom of the stairs—was installed, the open houses drew more visitors inside to view the home.

Notes

Chapter 8
Feng Shui the Area
Around Your Home

The key things to consider in the area around your home include the pathway to the front door, the driveway and the Bagua balance of the lot.

Ideally, the pathway to the front door is unobstructed, meandering and attractive, to welcome both support and energy to the home (Fig. 46).

To create an inviting entry, begin with clearing things along the pathway to the front door, such as over-hanging bushes and plant-

Fig. 46. Meandering
Entry Pathway

ings, children's toys or overgrowth at the edge of the walkway. To improve the appearance of the area in front of the door, place pots with plants and flowers, lighting or decorative items.

For a home with a straight pathway to the front door, place plantings, lights or pots that alternate along the path to create a meandering effect (Fig. 47). Fix any deterioration in the concrete or stone along the pathway, including broken or cracked steps.

The driveway is analyzed for its welcoming quality or problems with loss of energy. The driveway can be

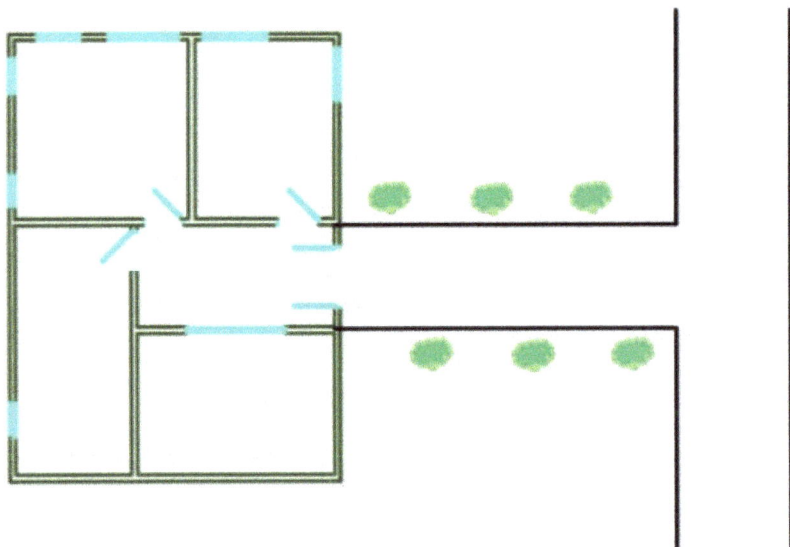

Fig. 47. Pathway Cure

improved in a similar way to the entry path by clearing or removing obstructions along the edge of the driveway.

A driveway that slants downward from the garage to the street can drain or block resources from the home, as well as diminish support for the home sale process. It is adjusted most often by placing larger objects like driveway pillars, rocks, or planters with flowers at the end of each side of the driveway. This helps hold energy in the property, as well as direct energy to the property. Placing lights, plants, or potted flowers along the driveway can help reduce the drain-out, as well as invite energy to the home.

When the incoming driveway travels past the house and the space ahead of it is unobstructed, it reduces resources coming into the home by guiding them past the house (Fig. 48).

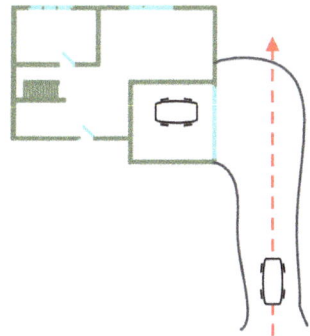

Fig. 48. Driveway Run-thru

Planting trees and placing large rocks or objects in the pathway of that energy will interrupt the Run-thru flow and redirect the energy toward the home (Fig. 49).

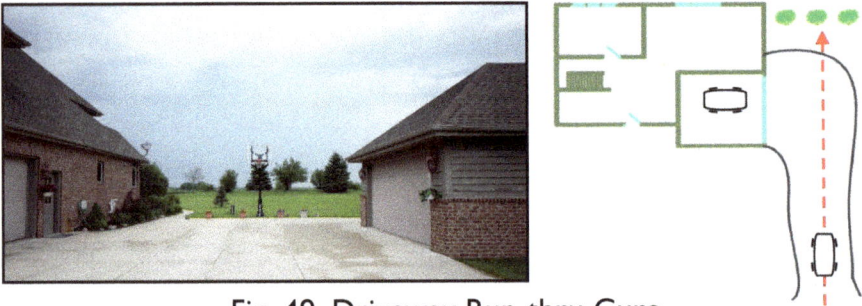

Fig. 49. Driveway Run-thru Cure

As with the home floor plan, the Bagua is placed over the layout of the entire property to determine if there are Missing Areas, Extensions, energetic imbalances or issues in Life Areas.

A Missing Area (Fig. 50) or Extension (Fig. 51) can occur when the lot is an irregular shape. Installing a light, planting trees and bushes, or placing a storage shed or other large objects along the boundary of a Missing Area can reduce its effect. Energizing the area opposite an Extension will bring balance to the lot. Objects such as trees, rocks, gardens, sculptures or out-buildings, and

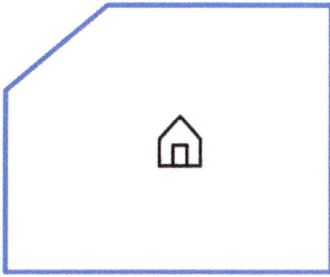

Fig. 50. Lot with
Missing Area

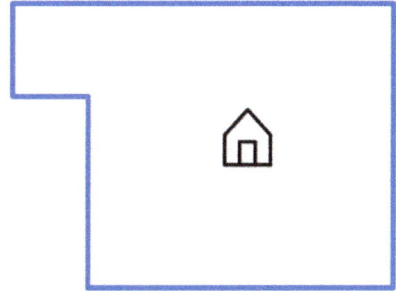

Fig. 51. Lot with Extension

active elements, such as kids play areas or bird-feeding spots, can energize an area opposite an Extension.

In the case where the shape of the lot is regular, these same items can create energetic imbalances if the areas opposite them are empty. These instances can be modified by installing another energetic item in the empty space. For example, if you have a large tree in the Wealth Area and the Helpful People Area is empty, you could set up a bird-feeding area in the empty space.

If you have a swimming pool, fountain or other water element in the Fame Area of the lot, you are bringing water to a Fire Area in the Bagua. This can negatively affect how buyers see your home. In this case, place some form of the wood element (plants, bushes, trees, wooden and/or

rectangular objects or the color green) near or around the water with the intent to absorb the water. (See Destructive Cycle, Fig. 32 on page 41.)

If the water element is larger, in the case of a swimming pool, a Bagua mirror may be needed, directed at the pool with the intent to "disappear" the effect of the water. (See Appendix A.) Alternatively, a regular mirror can be placed somewhere in the Wealth or Relationship Area of the lot facing the pool with the intent to pull the water element out of the Fame Area.

If the land in a Life Area goes significantly downhill, it could negatively affect goals in that area. Frequently, this occurs in the back of a lot, where it would affect Wealth,

Fame or Relationship by draining money from the home sale or reducing attention to the property. To cure this, place large objects, including rocks, trees or construction (out-building, stone fence, sculpture) at the beginning of a steeper incline and anywhere along an incline that has a more gradual drop-off.

If a property is adjacent to a freeway, a street with fast-moving vehicles, a rapid river, or a railroad track, it can be affected by their fast-moving *chi*, which pulls energy from the property. The best way to manage this is by creating a barrier that separates the property from the effect of the street, river, or railroad. Barriers in the form of trees, shrubs, plantings, large rocks or out-buildings can be effective. A FOR SALE sign placed perpendicular to the pulling energy flow can also help to slow it down.

At times, electrical and cellular poles and towers, along with transformers, can affect the property. Properties next to cemeteries, disruptive commercial property, a Shar chi or difficult neighbors can sometimes benefit from the use of a Bagua mirror to send away any negativities associated with them. (See Appendix A for how to use a Bagua mirror.)

Ideally, the FOR SALE sign is placed in the Helpful People Area of the lot, energizing the assistance of everyone involved in the home sale process. If that area lacks visibility or creates an imbalance in the property, the sign can be placed in the Knowledge or Career areas of the Bagua.

Sometimes, a FOR SALE sign may have enough red color, representing the Fire element, in it to make it detrimental to the Career Area of the lot, which is ruled by the Water element. Placing rocks (Metal element) around the base of the sign will reduce the effect of the fire.

In addition to drawing attention to the property, flags placed on the lot can be used to energize different parts of the Bagua. Pay attention to the color of the flag. For example, a blue flag, representing water, should not be placed in the Fame (fire) area. A red, bright yellow, or orange flag is better for activating that area.

Chapter 9
Cures, Intentions and Enhancements

CURES

A Feng Shui cure is used to adjust Run-thrus and Structural or Energetic imbalances, to modify negative effects, and to carry a home seller's intention. Some common Feng Shui cures include crystals, lights, live or silk plants, fountains, and rocks or stones. The following are sample circumstances in which cures are applied.

- A Run-thru can be cured by placing plants or objects along the pathway.

- An Energetic Imbalance is cured by raising the energy of the less active room by hanging a crystal or placing a light in that room.

- A light or a fish tank can be used to energize a room opposite an Extension to cure a Structural imbalance.

- The negative effect of an angled wall can be cured by hanging one or more pictures on the wall.

Choosing which cure to use depends on how severe the issue is. For example, how big is the Missing Area or Extension, and how active or inactive is the space you are balancing?

The bigger or more active an Extension is, the more energized the cure should be. For example, if the Extension contains a busy kitchen, a good cure might be a torchier lamp on a timer for three hours a day. If the Extension contains a quiet study, the opposite area could be cured with a small water fountain.

A large Missing Area might call for a larger-sized crystal cure. For example, a 50mm crystal could be installed when normally a 40mm one would be sufficient. A 30mm crystal might be used in the case of a small bathroom. A long Run-thru hallway may need more than one crystal, plant, or object.

INTENTIONS

Along with curing an issue, a cure can also carry the home seller's intention for the Life Area in which the cure is placed. The intention is energized by focusing on it during the cure installation process. To energize your intention further, write it down and place it somewhere in the Life Area of the cure. The note can be written on a small piece of paper and placed inconspicuously under a book, lamp, piece of furniture, or behind a painting.

Some common intentions for the home sale are:

- To sell quickly

- To sell for more money

- To sell easily

- To have people be helpful during the process

- To have the timing of the sale fit well for transitioning from one house to another

- To pass home inspection

- To prepare the home for showings well

The Intention Reinforcement Ritual (see Appendix B) is always used when installing cures in *situations that are problematic* or *include difficult issues,* such as when the home has been on the market for a while and has had very few showings, or when a buyer's financing is falling through.

ENHANCEMENTS

Enhancements are used to bring clarification and focus to the homeowner's intention relating to the home sale. Enhancements are not used to adjust energy like cures are. They are to be used after the home has been harmoniously balanced with cures. They will be less effective when added to a home that is not properly balanced.

For example, to enhance a homeowner's intention to sell a home more profitably, a symbol of prosperity, such as a crystal vase, could be placed in the Wealth Area. An intent to have helpful people involved in the home sale process could be enhanced by placing business cards of professionals who will be working with you (such as realtors or lending agencies) in the Helpful People Area. Placing an informational flyer in the Fame Area of the home could enhance the intent to draw the attention of more buyers to the property.

Elements can be used as enhancements. Representations of the Fire element, like red-colored objects, triangular-shaped items, and candles can be used to highlight the Fame Area, because it is a Fire element area. Plants and pictures of trees and flowers can also be enhancing because the Wood element feeds the Fire element. (See Creative Cycle, Fig. 31 on page 41).

In a family home, it may be beneficial for the sale to enhance the Health and Family area with representations of the Wood element, like plants, green items or rectangular shapes.

It is also enhancing to write out your intention on a piece of paper and place it in the Life Area that it applies to.

We have found that writing down your intention or goal in a question format is more successful in actually manifesting what you want. If you desire a quick sale, the question might read, "What would it take for me to sell my home quickly?" If you would like to attract a buyer who will appreciate the home, the question might might say, "What would it take to sell my home to someone who can really enjoy it?"

The question format allows for the focus on intention and facilitates the letting-go process so that goals can be more easily accomplished. Don't attempt to answer the "what would it take..." question, just let go.

Artwork that relates to the Life Area that it's in can be used as an enhancement, as long as it is placed with intention and relates positively to the Life Area in some way. For example, a painting of children playing in the Children and Creativity Area would be a good choice for attracting a buyer with children. Existing artwork should be removed or replaced if it detracts from a particular Life Area or intent. For example, a painting of a solitary person in the Relationship Area should be moved if you want to attract couples or families to the home.

Notes

....

....

....

....

....

....

....

....

....

....

....

....

....

....

Chapter 10
Feng Shui Plus

Here are some other helpful ideas that can be used along with Feng Shui when preparing a home for sale.

SPACE CLEARING

At times, using Space Clearing can be useful and productive to clear and refresh the area inside the home. You might also want to clear a space when there have been more serious issues like a death, arguments, illness, or emotional stresses in the home. Oftentimes, bells, drums and other sound instruments are used for the process.

The Epsom Salt Cleanse has shown clarifying and calming results and is something you can do yourself at home. To prepare, obtain a heat-resistant pan and place ¼ cup of Epsom salts in the center of the pan. Saturate the salts with rubbing alcohol. Set the pan in the center of each room to be cleared and ignite the mixture with a lighter or a match, allowing it to burn until the flame dies out. Refill for each room. You can also carry the pan around the room and reach into corners for a more thorough cleansing.

Consider using a hot pad or some protection from the heat. At times, you might also want to consider hiring a professional space clearer to produce more of the results you are after.

NUMEROLOGY

In some cases, it can be helpful to look at the numerology of the home address to create marketing and staging for the home that is in sync with its energy, character, and the type of buyer who would be attracted to it. For example, 5020 (add the address digits together 5+2) E. Olive St. would be a number 7 house, which resonates with the tone of rest and relaxation and is well suited to buyers who are looking for a retreat or place to retire. It could be marketed as "a place to get away from it all." An address of 3214 River Road has a 1 numerology (3+2+1+4=10   1+0=1). A #1 house can be appealing to buyers with a green thumb and could be marketed as such.

The book *Addresses Count* by Maryanna Korwitts offers a detailed evaluation of each house number and ideas on how to direct the marketing for your home sale.

STAGING

Quality staging is a valuable tool to use in conjunction with Feng Shui and is worth the investment. Remember that staging can affect the balance of energy in the home, so make Feng Shui adjustments accordingly.

ASTROLOGY

Consulting an astrologer can be helpful for choosing listing and closing dates. In general, it is advisable to avoid signing contracts during Mercury Retrograde periods. Consulting calendars that include the shadow periods is best. An astrologer can also help you look at when in general it is most optimal to plan a move.

Notes

....

....

....

....

....

....

....

....

....

....

....

....

....

....

....

....

....

....

....

....

Chapter 11
Additional Considerations

After the initial cures are installed, there may be some adjustments needed as things come up while your home is on the market. For example, you may need to tweak the Fame Area if your home is lacking in showings, or look at the Helpful People Area if there are troubles with the home inspection. Consider the balance of the Wealth Area if you are getting low-ball offers. Continue to fine-tune your cures and enhancements until your home or property has sold. Look for any results and changes to your goal areas to determine if adjustments are necessary to find the best balance.

On occasion, for various reasons, the homeowner or certain family members can be consciously or unconsciously resisting selling the home, which can block progress. For example, with a married couple, one of them might need to move for business reasons, and the other, though outwardly agreeing there is a need to move, inwardly holds on, not wanting to leave the neighborhood. Or perhaps there's an elderly parent who is reluctant to move to assisted living, or there are grown children who are resistant to selling the family homestead. This can manifest as not wanting to complete cures in certain areas or installing cures incorrectly.

It is helpful for the owner to imagine any areas where that kind of withholding might be occurring and talk about it with someone to release any blocks.

In real-life settings, there may occasionally be a home where Feng Shui results occur differently than expected. This invites looking beyond the basic considerations covered in this book. For example, in a home with a missing Wealth Area, owners had a positive financial situation instead of money problems. On further study, it was found that the Missing Area was balanced by the dynamic energy of the shape of the lot. Other considerations that go beyond basic Feng Shui are explored in our other books.

Using Feng Shui will influence your sale process in a positive way. However, the degree to which it can help also depends on a number of other factors like the expertise of your realtor, the current market, home price, and neighborhood. Other influences such as your astrology, karma, luck cycle, psychological blocks, cosmic flows, and unconscious intentions all have their own impacts.

Appendix A
Feng Shui Cures

Appendix B
Intention Reinforcement

Notes

Appendix A
Feng Shui Cures

Feng Shui cure is used to adjust Run-thrus and Structural or Electrical imbalances, to modify negative effects, and to carry a homeowner's intention. The following list includes some of the cures that are often used.

- Clear Crystal Balls (Fig. 52)
- Plants
- Lights
- Fountains
- Electrical Appliances
- Fish Tanks
- Heavy Objects
- Bagua Mirrors* (Fig. 53)
- Planter Pots
- Rocks and Stones
- Pinwheels
- Area Rugs
- Moving Objects
- Mobiles (Fig. 54)

Fig. 52. Crystal

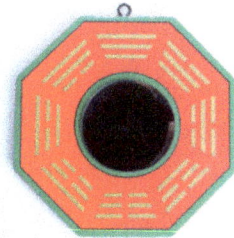

Fig. 53. Bagua Mirror

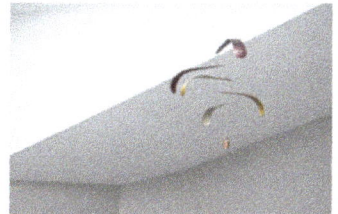

Fig. 54. Mobile

- Mirrors
- Wind chimes
- Fabric
- Corner Protectors
- Bird Feeders
- Trees
- Sculpture
- Flags

Please Note—Bagua Mirror:

Since the Bagua mirror can be very powerful, it is used only under special circumstances. It is used to send away potentially harmful energetic effects that may deter buyers, like large exterior Shars, (see Chapter 6) cemeteries, issues from problematic neighbors, freeways, cell towers, hospitals, and large commercial buildings. It is always directed toward something outside the home, not directed inside the home. The Bagua mirror can be placed inside as long as it is in a window or on an exterior wall facing outward.

It is important to use the Intention Reinforcement Ritual when installing a Bagua mirror, speaking aloud an intention specifically focused on sending away the negative effect of the item involved.

When purchasing a Bagua mirror, make sure to order regular Bagua mirrors, not concave or convex mirrors, which have special applications. When storing Bagua mirrors, they should be securely wrapped and placed facing downward.

ENHANCEMENTS

The following list includes some enhancements that can be used to focus your intentions:

- Artwork

- Pictures

- Figurines

- Meaningful items

- Notes with intentions

- Symbols for Wealth

The Five Elements are considered cures when they are correcting an elemental issue in a Life Area. Otherwise they are used to enhance a Life Area. The Five Elements are:

- **Earth**—Unglazed pottery, earth-tone colors, square items

- **Wood**—Flowers, trees, plants, green colors, rectangular forms

- **Fire**—Candles, lights, red, bright orange and yellow, triangular shapes

- **Water**—Water items like fountains, blue and black colors, wavy lines and objects

- **Metal**—Coins and other metal items, white and silver colors, circular shapes

Pictures or paintings of any of the items above can be representative of the element itself.

Installing Crystal Cures

Hang each crystal on a 3- to 9-inch red string or fishline 3 to 9 inches out from the corner of a room or away from the wall. With a Run-Thru, center the crystal in the pathway somewhere along its length. **Hang all of the crystal cures at the same time** to manage the change in energy evenly.

Remember to keep all the cures in place until you have closed the sale. Hang crystals using the Intention Reinforcement Ritual in Appendix B when there are specific real-life problems that are significant obstacles to the sale, like an issue with the home inspection or a lack of showings.

Appendix B
Intention Reinforcement Ritual

The Intention Reinforcement Ritual is used when installing a crystal cure to add strength to the cure. It is used when curing problematic or difficult situations, like continued lack of interest in a property. Focusing on the intention is what adds strength to the cure. The crystal then acts as an unconscious reminder of the intention. The intentions should relate to the Life Area in which the crystal is hung. Below are the steps to follow.

1. Consider any problems you have that relate to the Life Area of the Bagua. For example, low offers would relate to the Wealth Area. Potential buyers finding problem issues with the home would relate to the Helpful People or Fame & Reputation areas.

    Identify the problem(s) out loud and send the issue(s) away by using the flicking hand motion nine times. (Extend the two center fingers strongly past the resisting thumb to flick.) Direct the energy out of the home (Fig. 55).

2. Hang the crystal cure.

3. Recite nine times out loud, *"Om Mani Padme Hum."* This ancient mantra is pronounced "Ohm Mah Nee Pahd May Hum," and is used to enhance the cure with positive value.

Fig. 55—Flicking

4. Think about your intention as if you were living it right now. Get in touch with how it would feel if your intention had already manifested. Reach for the energy of what you want to create. Express out loud your intention in the best words possible. Some sample intentions might be:

- *Better offers are available more easily.*

- *Buyers find out about my property easily.*

- *People involved in the sale are helpful.*

- *Agents and buyers see value in my property.*

- *The home sale process goes quickly and easily.*

- *People feel at home visiting my house.*

- *Any issues that come up get resolved easily.*

5. Put your intention in the form of this question:
"What would it take…..?"

For example, "What would it take for buyers to see my home in a positive light?" Or, "What would it take to sell my home for the asking price?"

Remember to phrase questions so that everyone can benefit from the result.

Don't attempt to answer the question. Just let it go.

Please note:

It is important after completing the cure installation process to freely and completely let go, surrender, and turn your goals over to a higher power. Breathe, relax, accept, allow, and receive. Find activities that are relaxing and fun to shift your thoughts away from the desired outcome for a while.

About the Authors

Rhainey Watts-Cunningham and Alex Hartwell are certified Feng Shui professionals who have been practicing Feng Shui since 1998. They draw from extensive training in several different schools of Feng Shui, as well as professional practice in Psychotherapy and Counseling. A strong focus on intention and their personal practices in yoga, meditation, energy work, and astrology add dimension to what they do.

Using a team approach, they have found that focusing on certain key areas can serve to accomplish 90 percent of what a client wants from a Feng Shui consultation. Choosing these areas of focus makes looking at Feng Shui less complicated and more manageable. In these areas, they look at how to balance the energy of a home or property so that it facilitates the achievement of their clients' goals and intentions in areas such as Health, Wealth, Relationships, Career, Personal Growth, and Well-being.

Rhainey and Alex operate from the premise that the energy flow in a balanced home or property enhances the life and goals of the occupants. They offer corrections or cures to align the energy of a property with the owner's goals so that those goals unfold more easily.

Rhainey and Alex provide home and business consultations, evaluations for home sales and purchases, consultations for remodeling and building, as well as workshops and presentations. Through their writings, presentations and consulting practice, they intend to help people understand Feng Shui and its impact on their daily lives more easily.

Please contact the authors via their website:
www.DoorwaystoHarmony.com

www.ingramcontent.com/pod-product-compliance
Lightning Source LLC
Chambersburg PA
CBHW050018090426
42734CB00021B/3321